MW01004373

Forgiveness

RABBI RAMI
GUIDE TO

Forgiveness

- - - Roadside Assistance for the Spiritual Traveler - - -

Spirituality
&Health
BOOKS

Rabbi Rami Guide to Forgiveness:
Roadside Assistance for the Spiritual Traveler
By Rami Shapiro

© 2011 Rami Shapiro

425 Boardman Street, Suite C
Traverse City, MI 49684
www.spiritualityhealthbooks.com

All rights reserved. No part of this publication may be reproduced,
stored in a retrieval system, or transmitted in any form or by any
means without the prior written permission of the publisher.

Printed in Canada.

Cover and interior design by Sandra Salamony

Cataloging-in-Publication data for this book is available
upon request.

978-0-9837270-0-2
10 9 8 7 6 5 4 3 2 1

CONTENTS

INTRODUCTION 7

CHAPTER ONE: Thank God for Conflict 15

CHAPTER TWO: God Loves Conflict 23

CHAPTER THREE: No Choice 29

CHAPTER FOUR: Just Living 35

CHAPTER FIVE: Humility as the
Prelude to Forgiveness 43

CHAPTER SIX: What Is Your Purpose? 49

INTERLUDE 53

CHAPTER SEVEN: Forgiveness and
the Making of Meaning 61

CHAPTER EIGHT: What is Forgiveness? 69

CHAPTER NINE: Forgiveness and Freedom 83

CHAPTER TEN: Who Forgives Whom? 93

CHAPTER ELEVEN: The Three Questions 103

EPILOGUE: Forgiveness Month. 115

ABOUT THE AUTHOR 120

INTRODUCTION

SOME PEOPLE store grudges the way others store recipes.

My wife's grandmother used to keep little tin file boxes crammed with recipes: some neatly folded and others crushed and bent, some carefully printed out by hand in pen and pencil, others cut from magazines or torn from newspapers that yellowed with age. There seemed to be no order to her collection of recipes, though whenever she needed a specific recipe she knew exactly where to find it. Today's grandmothers may do something similar using a computer or iPad, and while the filing system may have changed, the passion for collecting, stuffing, and storing has not.

It is the same with grudges, slights, past hurts, and painful memories. We don't keep them in tin file card boxes or on digital flash drives, instead we cram them into our memory banks where, like our grandmother's recipes, they are easily retrieved when needed.

And when do we need them? Whenever we want to feel a bit holier-than-thou, cede to ourselves the moral high ground, or justify our recurring anger at one person or another.

Lest you think I'm not talking about you, try this little experiment: Take a moment and think back to the earliest memory you have of being hurt by someone you trusted, liked, or loved. If you are like most people, such memories are not difficult to recall.

For example, as soon as I ask myself this question, I remember being continually bullied by two sixth-grade girls when I was a third-grader at George Washington Elementary School in Springfield, Massachusetts. Seeing them knock me down on my way to school in the winter, stuff snow into my Charlie Brown cap with earflaps, and then jam the hat on my head so tightly that my scalp burns with the cold is like watching an old movie. I feel sorry for that kid, and even sorrier for those girls, but I am no longer that little boy, and if those little girls tried to do that to me today I'd scare them away. Assuming, of course, they were still twelve years old and I am my current age of sixty.

Time has muffled the pain, but the memory is not forgotten. Have I forgiven these tween terrorists? No. I moved past it simply because my dad made more

8

money than their dads, and we found a new house in the safer suburbs. In time I outgrew the Charlie Brown winter headwear, but not the bullying.

I remember a "friend" in the seventh grade who would back me against a wall and wail into my stomach with his fists clenched almost as tightly as his jaw. He was a good twelve inches shorter and nowhere near my weight. I never hit him back, but I would look down on him and say, "What the hell do you think you're doing?" After throwing a few more punches he would realize that he wasn't hurting me, and he would stop the pounding. I doubt he had a clue why he exploded this way or why I was his preferred target. I just kept the pounds on to protect myself from the pounding.

Did I forgive him for his brutality? No. One day he and his family just moved away. One less bully in our junior high school, but there were plenty more. I never forgave any of them. In fact, now that I am writing about this, I can't tell you one person whom I have forgiven. Nor can I explain what forgiving someone actually is.

I know the saying, "forgive and forget," but clearly I haven't forgotten and just as clearly I haven't forgiven. And while I would not be so smug as to claim that these and similar experiences don't shape the person I am today, I am smug enough to imagine that if they do, they do so only slightly.

So here I am writing the *Rabbi Rami Guide to Forgiveness* without the foggiest idea of what forgiveness is or how to go about forgiving people.

What I am good at, however, is asking for forgiveness. I am fairly attuned to the pain I cause others, so I am quick to ask. Yet, if I am honest, I must admit that asking for forgiveness is often a tactic for alleviating the guilt I feel when I cause another to suffer. If I can get you to forgive me, I can move on without carrying the guilt of having caused you unnecessary pain in the first place. And, if you are lucky, I may actually learn something from the experience and not cause you pain in the future. At least not the same pain.

I don't want to give you the impression that I'm hard hearted and never forgive people. I do, and I do it all the time. If you hurt me and ask for my forgiveness, I immediately smile, grant your request, and give you a hug. Then, when we part, I make a mental note never to trust you again.

It isn't that I cut off all ties with you. On the contrary, we may have a close and continuing relationship, but I no longer entertain the notion that you won't hurt me. Chances are you will, and chances are I will hurt you as well. So forgiveness, whatever it is, isn't the ending of hurt or the possibility of hurt. It is simply moving on a bit more wisely. Now that is a definition of forgiveness you won't find in any dictionary: "Forgiveness, verb, the act of moving on with your life a bit more wisely."

Forgiveness won't erase the past, but it just might free you from it; it won't save you from suffering, but it just might help you realize that suffering is simply part of the human condition, and thus allow you to suffer without the added element of surprise. Maybe forgiveness is simply the stripping away of illusion so that you can navigate your way through life with more clarity and less bruising.

I don't know, but I will take the notion that forgiveness is about living life more wisely as our operational definition for this *Guide*. If we discover it is something else along the way, all well and good. But I suspect we will refine rather than replace our definition. And, since I've read this book all the way to end, you can take my word that refining rather that replacing is exactly what we will do.

So let's be clear: this is a guide to forgiveness by a fellow whose definition of forgiveness differs from almost everyone else's, and who isn't in any way a master of the practice of forgiveness at all. So why should you read this book? Here are the three reasons for doing so.

First, most books on forgiveness assume forgiveness is a skill you can learn and use whenever you wish. I disagree. Forgiveness isn't a skill, but a level of understanding of the nature of life and how best to live it. It isn't something you can use the way you might use an umbrella or a fork, it is an attitude toward self and others and life in general that can be cultivated but never mastered.

Second, most books on forgiveness suggest that forgiveness is a way of escaping suffering; this one doesn't. Forgiveness isn't a tactic you can employ to make your life less stressful and more joyous. Forgiveness isn't something you can deploy to end suffering. Suffering is a part of life; the Buddha went so far as to say that suffering is life, or at least life is suffering when you continue to live it in a manner rooted in craving and grasping, and the anger, arrogance, and jealousy that erupts when you do live this way.

I don't think you can escape suffering, nor should you want to. Life is what it is: a blend of joy and sorrow, happiness and horror. Forgiveness won't change that. But it can free you from dragging the sorrow into your moments of joy, and allowing the horror to corrode your moments of happiness, and that is no small thing at all.

Third, most books on forgiveness offer you practical steps to achieve forgiveness; this one doesn't. While I would like to offer you a method, I can't find one that works for me, so I have none to offer you. Forgiveness just isn't that easy.

What we can do, and what we will do in this brief *Guide to Forgiveness*, is understand more deeply what forgiveness is and how forgiveness works. But more importantly, we will focus on who you are, who the people you hurt are, and who the people who hurt you are. We will delve into the nature of self and see that you aren't who you think you are, and when you stop thinking you are who you are not, forgiveness happens: no method, no steps, no willful thinking or feeling one way or another; just a freeing of Self from the confines of self and realizing that freedom from self manifests as forgiveness.

Of course there is more to this than playing with lower and uppercase *S*'s, and we will learn ways of shifting from self to Self and allowing forgiveness to arise of its own accord, but you will not be a master of forgiveness after reading this book. You'll thank me later.

CHAPTER ONE

Thank God for Conflict

YOUR LIFE IS A STORY you tell yourself and others. Notice how you respond the next time someone asks you, "How'd your day go?" Chances are you don't pull out a PowerPoint presentation with the highlights of your day laid out in bullet-points. Most likely you open with something catchy, either positive or negative, but in either case designed to rev you up to tell the story of your day and get your audience primed to listen.

You talk about the people you encountered, what they said, what you said in response to what they said, how they reacted to what you said in response to what they said, and on and on and on. You're telling a story. It may be a drama, a comedy, a tragedy, or a blend of all three. There are characters in your story, and plot twists, and sometimes flashbacks. Your life is no less compelling than any life portrayed on The Biography Channel, and you use the same tools screenwriters and film directors use to tell those stories. And because your life is a story, it needs conflict.

A story without conflict is boring. If there is no danger and nothing to overcome, if the characters have no stake in the play and its outcome, no one cares to listen and you probably don't care to tell it. In fact, you probably don't much care about living it. Life without conflict is no life at all.

What causes conflict? It's simple: you have a plan and nothing goes according to it. Now what do you do? You are dating the partner of a lifetime, only to find out you've been double-timed. You land the job of your dreams and your boss turns out to be an abusive SOB. Or your best friend gets cancer and dies. Or your parents abandon you. Or your sibling commits suicide. Or any number of horrible things that can happen to people happens to you. Now what do you do?

We imagine that we would prefer a life without conflict. But the fact is, without conflict we can't grow or develop character; without conflict we would find life meaningless.

Decades ago I was talking with my friend and spiritual mentor Father Thomas Keating. I was asking him about his years as a Trappist monk before Vatican II, when the monks lived in silence. At the time, I romanticized silence.

Growing up in a traditional Jewish home, silence was anathema: "What? You're not talking? You're too important to say hello to your mother?" Even when our prayer books instructed us to pray silently, we were taught to mumble the prayers aloud. Being raised in a world of babble, I assumed silence would allow us to move deeply inward, to cleanse ourselves of shallow desires and ego-centrism. I longed to go on silent retreats and imagined that a life of silence would be a life of bliss.

Father Thomas taught me otherwise. The monks would hang chalkboards on cords around their necks so they could write to one another. "You would be amazed," Father Tom said to me, "just how much jealousy and anger one learns to cram into one of those tiny slates."

Conflict doesn't require verbal speech. Conflict

only requires other people. Perhaps the best way to avoid conflict, and hence the need to forgive and be forgiven, would be to avoid other people. I've tried it. It doesn't work.

I have gone on solitary retreats, living alone for periods of time in small cells in monasteries and ashrams and in tiny huts in the mountains. I have meditated, chanted, and walked silently for hours all by myself, but as long as there is a self there is conflict as well.

It turns out that I am never really solitary because I am not really singular. My mind is filled with differing voices and personalities arguing with one another over who I am and what I am to do and how I am to do it. There is as much potential for conflict within my own mind as there is between my mind and your mind. It turns out we don't need anyone to make us miserable or anxious or angry or fearful—we are capable of generating all the conflict we need to fuel all the stories we will ever tell all by ourselves.

Years ago I was a student of Psychosynthesis, a school of psychology created by Roberto Assagioli (1888–1974). I was taught that I am a composite being made up of a variety of conflicting subpersonalities— aspects of myself that seem to have a life of their own, who battle with other aspects of myself to define just who I am and what I am to do with my life. Whenever you find yourself arguing with yourself, you're dealing with subpersonalities.

Part of my training was learning how to work with these subpersonalities in a way that allowed each to have a vote but none to have a veto when it comes to who I am and how I am to live. I learned to convene a board meeting of the key subpersonalities that comprised my psyche: the CEO, CFO, Secretary, Father, Son, Brother, Husband, Teacher, Rabbi, etc. While each subpersonality is an aspect of myself, I consciously played the role of the CEO, convening the meeting, setting the agenda, and then asking each attendee to give his particular take on the issue. As I made room for each voice, I discovered that I was conflicted on many of the challenges I was facing. There was no one right way for me to respond; and the idea of being true to my self really meant listening to multiple selves and then negotiating among them to come up with some plan of action. While there is much more to Psychosynthesis than this, I continue to find this exercise helpful, especially when it comes to matters of conflict.

EXERCISE #1: **COME TO MEETING**

Sit comfortably and close your eyes. Imagine you are in a boardroom, sitting at the head of a formal meeting table. Joining you for this meeting are five others (if there are more, fine, but keep the number manageable), each representing one key role you play in life. Invite each attendee to introduce herself and briefly articulate her function: parent, partner, spouse, child, etc.

Now explain the situation you are wrestling with and ask each representative to share her understanding of the situation and how best to handle it. Don't interrupt or allow others to interrupt. Just listen to each respondent and become aware of the inner conflict you may have around this issue. If you wish to negotiate a settlement, listen to conflicting voices and seek common ground and compromise. Agree to disagree on those issues upon which you cannot find common ground, and then make a decision as CEO, assuring all in attendance that you will convene another meeting after

the decision has been implemented to see how
things are going.

For the purposes of this *Guide*, the point of this
exercise is simply to realize that conflict is natural to
life and that imagining you can escape from it into
some interior perfection is nonsense. Nor is it wise
to pretend that conflict is the fault of others. Rather
conflict is systemic to life, which means that hurting
and being hurt are also part of the way things are, and
no amount of forgiveness will erase this. Forgiveness
is not a one-time act, but an ongoing attitude rooted
in the realization that conflict is as natural to living as
breathing.

CHAPTER TWO

God Loves Conflict

I AM AN ADJUNCT PROFESSOR of religious studies at Middle Tennessee State University. My students and I often get into deep philosophical discussions on the nature of God, and one of the most common beliefs people seem to have is that God is all-knowing. God knows exactly what you will do from the moment you gasp your first breath until the moment you sigh your last. It isn't that God predetermines what you will do (though some of my students believe that as well), but being omniscient, God knows the future.

Many students find this belief comforting. While it is often my business (as well as my pleasure) to discomfit my students, when this particular subject comes up I shift the conversation to what it must be like to be all-knowing. I can't help but feel sorry for an omniscient God.

An all-knowing God lives in a world of endless reruns. Since everything that will happen is already known, there is no surprise. God watches your life unfold without much interest because God already knows how it will unfold. Not only does God know the big things, but the minute ones as well.

When I watch *The Mentalist*, one of my favorite television shows, I know that the crime will be solved and lots of soap will be sold in just under an hour. But I take delight in what the characters say and how the plot twists one way or another, and I love trying to figure out who did it before the characters tell me who the murderer is. But if I knew the dialogue by heart, if I knew every twist and counter twist before it even happens, the show would hold no interest for me. In fact, I wouldn't pay any attention to it.

So now imagine God—the all-knowing, never to be surprised God—spending eternity watching shows committed to memory eons before they ever see the light of day. Boring. If God is dead, as some philosophers insist, I suspect God died of boredom.

What God wants is what we want: surprise. Things

shouldn't go as planned. That is when things get interesting. That is when things become fun. And that is when conflict enters the picture.

The best kind of conflict for us humans is human conflict. While it is true that I enjoy playing Scrabble against the computer on my iPad, I never begrudge the program when it takes advantage of my mistakes. Nor do I get much pleasure in beating the computer, which I do more often than not. (I avoid the *Hard* setting.) It never occurs to me to challenge a word the computer chooses or to stick my face close to the screen and yell, "Gotcha!" when I manage to use all of my letters to form a single word.

But when I play with a human partner, watch out.

Conflict is natural and to be welcomed. Yes, without conflict we would never have to forgive or be forgiven, but we would hardly be alive. Forgiveness matters because conflict happens. And real conflict happens when the people you love the most treat you like crap, and vice versa.

The first thing you need to know about forgiveness is that it depends upon conflict, and conflict is what makes life worth living, so not only might you consider forgiving those who hurt you, but you might

25

also consider thanking them for doing so. Otherwise you'd have no story, and without a story you have no life.

EXERCISE #2: **THANK THE BASTARDS**

Make a list of everyone who has hurt you: really, everyone. Think back as far as you can remember in your life, and make a list. Write down their names, what they did, and how it has impacted you. When you have completed your list, imagine what your life would have been like if none of these things ever happened to you. Don't focus on just the terrible horrors—abuse, rape, murder of a loved one—we could all do without these. But imagine if nothing hurtful ever happened to you. What would you be like? Write a thank you note to each of the people on your list. Let them know what you learned from their behavior and how you have grown from the hurt they caused you. Try not to be sarcastic. Living well is the best revenge.

26

It may well be that you just can't bring yourself to write a thank-you note to some of the people on your list. Don't worry about it; skip them. You needn't mail these notes anyway. The act of writing them is what matters, for doing so will help you realize that you have grown from all these sorrows, and that is the point.

Character is built through adversity. As the nineteenth-century German philosopher Friedrich Nietzsche wrote in his book *Twilight of the Idols*, "What does not kill me, makes me stronger." Like any other muscle, the muscle of character is developed through resistance.

A few years ago I wrote a book on how to use "The Twelve Steps of Alcoholics Anonymous" as a general spiritual practice. This "Thank the Bastards" exercise is the opposite of Step 8. In Step 8 we make "a list of all people we had harmed, and became willing to make amends to them all." In this forgiveness exercise the list is reversed. This is a list of people you imagine *owe you* an apology, not the other way around.

When I made my list of people who have hurt me I discovered something interesting. The people who hurt me the most were people I love the most. I'm not

27

saying that these were people I loved in the past and whom I ceased to love when they caused me pain. I'm saying that the people who caused me pain in the past are often people I still love in the present.

I don't love them because they caused me pain; I'm not a masochist. Nor do I love them in spite of their causing me pain; I'm not a saint. I just still love them. And when I think about those moments when they hurt me, I discover through that love something else: they didn't have a choice.

CHAPTER THREE

No Choice

WHEN SOMEONE HURTS US we tend to think they could have done otherwise. In fact if we don't assume this, we wouldn't have the moral high ground from which to be hurt and bestow forgiveness. But is this really true? Can people do other than they do?

During my twenty years as a congregational rabbi, I have spoken with lots of people who felt betrayed by a spouse or life-partner. The conversation usually went like this:

"Rabbi, how could she sleep with someone else? She must have known how much it would hurt me."

"Why did she sleep with him?"

"She says she loves him."

"If she loves him, how could she not sleep with him?"

"What!"

"Look, when you fell in love with her, didn't you want to sleep with her? Didn't it dominate your every waking thought when you were together? Did you go about it rationally, or did your emotions and hormones just drive you to it?"

"But we're married."

"So that means she's no longer driven by passion?"

"Exactly."

"People don't operate that way. Look, it certainly would have been better for you if she never met this guy, but she did, and she fell in love with him, and I guarantee you that at the moment she made love to him she wasn't thinking about you or your kids or what it would do to anyone else but her at that moment. She wasn't trying to hurt you, but to pleasure herself."

"You really aren't making things better, Rabbi."

"Oh, you want better? I didn't know. Anyway, I have no idea how to make it better. We'd have to go back in time and leave pictures of you and your kids on the bed in their motel room. I have no idea how to time travel. The only question for you is this: what will you do now?"

I wasn't all that good at counseling people.

I think people are fairly simple: we want to be happy and will do lots of stupid things to make ourselves happy. Most of these things don't work, and leave us with messes to clean up. Sometimes we act like adults and clean up those messes. Most often we act like little kids and leave them for someone else to clean up. But rarely do we set out to make a mess. We set out to be happy, and it is the quest for happiness that makes the mess.

EXERCISE #3:
MESS MAKER, MESS MAKER, MAKE ME A MESS

Think of the last three times you hurt people. Write down what you did and why it caused another to suffer. Now write down your motive for doing what you did. Be honest: did you deliberately set out to hurt the other person? Or were you pursuing some other goal, some personal happiness or pleasure, and the person you hurt was collateral damage?

31

Most people don't set out to deliberately hurt you. Most people aren't sociopaths. Most people get caught up in the pursuit of happiness and are as surprised as you are when their pursuit causes you pain. So should you abandon your pursuit of happiness and instead set out to make yourself miserable? No, that wouldn't change things much. You would just make different messes and always for the same reason: you set out in pursuit of something.

When you set out to make yourself happy (or miserable if you prefer), you have to control those around you. You have to script a play, and convince or force others to play the parts you have written for them. This rarely works. People refuse to read their lines or take their places or let you have your way. They have their own scripts from which they want you to read, and they have committed themselves to their own preferred outcomes. It is just a mess.

But there is an alternative: stop trying to script your life, and just go about living it.

What about the fellow whose wife cheated on him? He couldn't forgive her. In fact she never even asked him for forgiveness. She was in love with someone else and wanted a divorce. He gave her that, but the separation was legal and physical but never emotional. He carried her with him into every new relationship he had. He couldn't forgive. He couldn't forget. And worse, he couldn't move on.

"I can't trust anyone," he said to me on a later occasion. "I think every woman I meet is going to cheat on me. Is that crazy?"

"Not at all. Your experience tells you that is a real possibility."

"You mean they are going to cheat on me?"

"I mean you can't know in advance if they are going to cheat on you or not. This situation isn't unique to you. Nobody can be sure that the person they love won't cheat on them."

"That can't be right. I didn't believe my wife could cheat on me."

"And you were wrong. All I'm saying is that no matter what we tell ourselves about other people— people we love, people we hate—what they do and what we say about them have nothing to do with one another. Think what you want, people will still do what they do."

"If I can't trust someone, I can't love them."

"Then I guess you're done with love."

33

"You are not being helpful at all, Rabbi!"

"Look, these are your rules, not mine. You're saying that you can no longer trust anyone. And you're saying that if you can't trust someone you can't fall in love with him or her. All I'm saying is that if these two things are true, then you are done with love."

"Then what should I do?"

"Change the rules, and stop making trust a requirement for love. Love is a risky business. You don't choose whom to fall in love with; that is why it is called *falling* in love rather than rationally thinking your way into love. When you fall in love you can't know how it will turn out. So you either try to divine the future before acting, or you realize that you cannot know in advance what will happen with this relationship and you just dive in anyway. The only thing you can be sure of is that, however things turn out, they won't be the way you imagine in advance. So the choice is simple: just live your life with not-knowing, letting joy and suffering play themselves out, or don't live at all."

My counseling skills did not improve over time.

CHAPTER FOUR

Just Living

WHAT DOES IT MEAN to just live your life? Am I suggesting you have no plan, no dream, and no preferences as to what happens to you and those you love? Not at all. Planning, dreaming, and having preferences are natural, and they are no more yours to control than the actions of those you love. All I am suggesting is that even as you plan and dream and desire this over that, just remind yourself that you have no control over any of it.

This issue of control, or our lack of it, often gets me in trouble. We want to believe we are in charge of our lives. We want to believe that we can control our thoughts, and think ourselves to happiness. I once took a seminar entitled "You Are Only a Thought Away from Happiness." True enough, but eight hours and far too many dollars later, I still had no idea how to control that elusive thought.

I've read *The Secret* and watched the movie, and I understand that my thoughts create my future: think good, get good; think bad, get bad. I'm not saying this is true, but it sounds easy enough, and easy often trumps truth, so let's go with easy for a moment. If I control my thinking I will "manifest" the world I want. Great.

At least it sounds great until I realize that most of my thinking happens in my subconscious mind beyond the control of my conscious ego. According to the *think good, get good* theory, the universe will respond to my thoughts and do my bidding just like the genie in the story of Aladdin. The problem is that by the time I know I'm thinking negatively, I have already thought negatively and the universe is gearing up to dump a whole lot of negative on me. Even if I quickly shift gears and try to ward off the negative with lots of positive, the thought that I am doing this to stave off the negative actually causes the universe to dump even more negativity on me. I'm screwed!

The truth is you can't control your thoughts. Yes, you can deliberately think about one thing or another, but you cannot avoid thoughts you don't want to think.

Furthermore, you don't even know you have unwanted thoughts until you have already thought them. Go ahead, make a mental list of all the thoughts you don't want to think. Uh-oh. You've just thought them!

Now I'm not the first person to realize this. In fact, one of the talking heads in *The Secret* movie makes the same point. The solution, we are told, is to focus on feelings. You can tell how you are thinking by how you are feeling, and you can control your thinking by controlling your feelings. Forget *think good, get good* and focus on *feel good, get good* instead.

Unfortunately, this doesn't help much at all. First of all, if I'm feeling bad that means I'm thinking negatively, and if I'm thinking negatively the universe is out to get me which only makes me feel worse. And, secondly, I can no more control my feelings than I can my thoughts.

If you could control your feelings you wouldn't ever feel sad or angry or fearful or envious. You'd just feel joyous and glad and happy all the time. The fact is, however, that you don't feel this way all the time, and insisting you can and should is just setting yourself up for more failure and, hence, greater negativity.

You can't control your feelings for the same reason

37

you can't control my thoughts: feelings rise of their own accord without your conscious mind deciding one way or another. By the time your conscious mind knows what you're feeling, you're already feeling it. Your only choice is what to do with your thoughts and feelings once they are thought and felt, not whether or not to think or feel them in the first place. And even this is problematic.

EXERCISE #4: **WHO'S IN CHARGE?**

Point your right index finger at your nose. Whenever you feel like it, and completely at your own command, point that finger at your stomach instead.

Whether you did this exercise or not, you made a decision: "I am going to point my finger at my nose and shift it to my stomach, or I'm not. My choice." But is it? When you engage in some voluntary action, the prefrontal region of your brain sends messages to the premotor cortex, which in turn sends messages to the primary motor cortex, which in turn sends out the command to move your finger. But who initiates this?

In 1985, Benjamin Libet, a researcher at the University of California in San Francisco, discovered that your brain actually prepared to move your finger one third of a second prior to your conscious decision to move your finger. So did you consciously decide to move your finger or did you simply acquiesce to what was already happening in your brain?

You may not accept Libet's findings. I understand that. Accepting them seems to suggest that you are not in control; that you are not the boss of your own body and mind, and this can be troubling. After all, if you aren't in control of you, who is?

The answer I prefer is this: no one. That subjective experience I call "I" isn't independent of my physical sensations, emotions, and thoughts; it is an epiphenomenon that becomes conscious of them after the fact. I don't think my thoughts; my thoughts somehow think me.

Don't worry if you can't accept this. If you can control your thoughts, and you are not thinking of a naked skier racing down the slopes of Aspen as you read this sentence about a naked skier racing down the slopes of Aspen, I'm impressed. And if you don't feel even a little annoyed that I just tricked you into

39

thinking something you didn't want to think about, I'm even more impressed. Me? I'm annoyed and I knew it was coming.

I'm raising this issue in the context of forgiveness for one reason: if you aren't really in control of what you think and feel, and if even your actions are somehow beyond your conscious control, how can you weave your epic tales of woe that make forgiveness so important in the first place?

Earlier today Murphy, my goldendoodle, knocked over a glass of juice I had placed on my coffee table. Her tail just hit the glass as she stood next to me hoping for a bite of egg. The spilled juice ruined my breakfast and stained the carpet. Did I get angry with her? Yes, for a moment. Did the anger last? No, because I knew that she doesn't control the wagging of her tail. Am I saying that what is true of Murphy's tail is true of our actions as well? Yes and no.

Yes, in the sense that we do most of what we do without thinking through the potential consequences. And no, in that we do have some capacity for fore-thought, and should learn to use it. But, yes, again, because most of the time when we do act we don't even think there will be consequences, so we don't think about thinking ahead. And no, again, because we should now know there are always consequences and so we should always think ahead. But then, yes, because even if we know this intellectually we don't know it consciously all the time, but . . . You get the idea. We can't say the tail wags the dog, but we can't say the dog wags the tail either. All we can say is that tail wagging happens, and sometimes so does spilled juice.

CHAPTER FIVE

Humility as the Prelude to Forgiveness

IF WE CAN'T CONTROL our thoughts and feelings, if thoughts and feelings are just going to pop up often in ways that are totally inappropriate, if tails wag and juice spills, and we really can't do much about any of this, how then shall we live? Humbly.

I have attended a number of silent meditation retreats. I enjoy the quiet and the stillness, and I suffer the conceit that I am spiritual. Years ago I went on one of these retreats where, in addition to silence, no eye contact was allowed. I arrived after the general introductions were made, and so I never spoke with

43

or even saw the people with whom I was meditating.

The very first morning I'm sitting cross-legged on my meditation cushions, my eyes slightly open and staring unfocused on the floor about eighteen inches in front of me. Out of the corner of my eye I notice a man wearing black sweatpants sitting cross-legged to my right. All I know about him is that he is wearing black sweatpants. I don't know his race, his age, his occupation, his sexual preference, his politics, or whether or not he has a family or a criminal record. All I know is that he is wearing a pair of black sweatpants identical to the pair I am wearing. Oh, that and one other thing: I hate him.

Seriously, I hated him. There was something about those black sweatpants, bent at the knee pretty much like mine, that just made me furious. Maybe I hated him because he had chosen to wear the same pants, and I was hoping to make a fashion statement at the retreat. I really don't know. All I know is that my feelings toward this man, or at least his calves, dominated my thinking for days.

Meditation retreats cost too much money to waste time critiquing some faceless fellow's outerwear, and yet here I was doing just that. But I did learn something:

44

I'm not in control of my thoughts and feelings. It was, and still is every time I think of it, humbling. And that's a good thing.

When I know I can't control my thoughts and feelings, I stop blaming myself for what I think and feel, and I stop insisting that other people control their thoughts and feelings as well. And when I stop insisting that other people control their thoughts and feelings, I stop expecting them to think and feel the way I do or the way I wish them to think and feel. I simply expect them to think and feel, and to be as surprised and humbled by their thoughts and feelings as I am by my own, though this, too, is outside my control.

All this is very liberating. Humility is freeing. Knowing that thoughts and feelings just happen allows me to just think and feel without judging anyone, myself included. To paraphrase Jesus, "Let he who is without a crazy thought cast the first stone."

EXERCISE #5: **CULTIVATING HUMILITY**

Set one day aside this week to just observe your thoughts and feelings. Notice how they rise and fall of their own accord. More importantly, notice how often they are really

inappropriate. Someone is telling you a very
sad story, and you think of a very funny joke.
Or you see a very attractive stranger and you
suddenly feel a flush of sexual arousal. Or
you are walking through a restaurant and
see something delicious on a stranger's plate
and the urge to grab it and eat it suddenly
dominates your consciousness for a moment.
Take note of how insane your mind really is.
And let that realization humble you.

I was first introduced to the madness of mind and
its centrality to humility by David K. Reynolds, Ph.D.,
the founder of Constructive Living, an approach to
life that blends two distinct Japanese therapies, Morita
and Naikan. Naikan focuses on the cultivation of
gratitude and is discussed at length in the forthcoming *Rabbi Rami Guide to Gratitude*. Morita deals more
with how we respond constructively to life, regardless
of our thoughts and feelings about life.

Dr. Shoma Morita (1874–1938) was a Japanese
psychiatrist and academic who created his system
of therapy around the same time as Sigmund Freud
and Carl Jung were creating theirs. Where Freud and

Jung sought to lessen our neurotic symptoms, Morita sought to cultivate strength of character that would allow us to act responsibly regardless of our thoughts and feelings. "Trying to control the emotional self willfully by manipulative attempts is like trying to choose a number on a thrown dice," Morita taught. And your failure to do so only aggravates your situation.

Rather than control your mind, learn to accept it. Rather than set out to think only certain thoughts and feel only certain feelings, learn to accept whatever thoughts and feelings arise. Yet, just as you cannot control them, you need not let them control you.

As Dr. David Reynolds puts it, the goal of Morita therapy is threefold: know your purpose, accept your feelings, and do what must be done. We have been talking about acceptance, now let us focus a bit on purpose and doing.

CHAPTER **SIX**

What Is
Your Purpose?

PURPOSE CAN BE GREAT OR SMALL. You can set out to cure cancer or wash your car. In either case, chances are that your thoughts and feeling will often be at odds with that purpose.

I have never had a passion for medicine, and curing cancer was never a prime motivator for me. Of course if I stumble over a cure, I would certainly share it with the world, but I would never set out to actually discover it. I have often had the desire to wash my car. Or, if not the desire, at least the need. My next-door neighbor has a passion for birdhouses and has a dozen or so strung up along the side of her home that parallels my driveway. They attract a lot of birds, and my car attracts a lot of their droppings. So the need to wash my car is fairly constant.

Yet I rarely do so. Why? I think it is going to rain. Or I just don't feel like it. It does rain sometimes, and I really never feel like washing the car, but there are times when it just has to be done. So I do it. I don't do it gladly or happily. I do it grumpily, with an eye out for my neighbor that I might mention what a mess her beloved birdhouses cause. I don't forgive my neighbor for hanging the birdhouse, or the birds for crapping on my car. I just wash the car.

And guess what?—it gets clean. And when it is clean I actually feel good about it. I didn't wash the car in order to feel good. I washed it because soon the driver-side door would be too encrusted with bird droppings to actually open. It had to be done, so, negativity and all, I did it. *Know your purpose*: have a clean car; *Accept your feelings*: my neighbor is a bitch, and she should be washing my car; *Do what must be done*: wash the damn car.

I realize washing bird crap off your car isn't the kind of purpose Pastor Rick Warren had in mind when he wrote his bestseller *The Purpose Driven Life*, but it is the best I could do. Pastor Rick begins his book by telling you "It's not about you," and that purpose that should drive your life is God's purpose for your life and not your purpose at all.

Dr. Morita was a Buddhist and didn't think of God this way, if in fact he thought of God at all. So when Dr. David Reynolds taught me about purpose, he wasn't thinking about God either. He was thinking about this moment.

EXERCISE #6: **THIS MOMENT, THIS PURPOSE**

Right now you are sitting and reading this *Guide*; that is your purpose for the moment. You may have other things that need doing, and not doing them may cause you to feel guilty or anxious, but you have decided to make reading this *Guide* a priority, so let the feelings alone and keep reading. Or, if what has to be done trumps sitting and reading, get up and do whatever is next. This is what life is: doing what needs doing this moment and the next. So take a moment and think about what really needs doing today. Make a list. Notice how you feel about doing these things: some you may like to do, others you may hate to do. Don't rank them by feelings, rank them by importance. Do the most important one first (assuming it can be done). Don't try and change your feelings regarding it, just do it.

What does this have to do with forgiveness? The more you do, the more you accomplish, the more constructive and productive your life, the less you will carry grudges and have to worry about forgiveness. Of course you will still screw up and have to ask others for forgiveness, but you will be too busy living to carry the burden of blame.

Be careful here: I am not saying that you should simply keep busy for busy's sake. I am not saying that you should run around frantically doing this and that to distract yourself from your feelings or from the hurt others have caused you. The doing I am talking about isn't busywork at all, but things you really need to do. All I am saying is this: the more you do what needs doing, the more productive your life becomes, the less time and energy you have to stew over the past, and fantasize over how others have stolen your present.

YOU ARE JUST about halfway through the *Rabbi Rami Guide to Forgiveness*, and if the second half of this book is going to make any sense to you, you had best be clear about what I have said in the first half. So let me take a few pages to recap.

First, life is wild, chaotic, uncontrollable, often ecstatically joyous, and just as often horribly painful. Second, you aren't in control of this wildness. Third, you aren't here to learn something, achieve something, or earn your way out to some better world. You are just here. While you're here you may learn a lot, achieve a lot, and when you do leave this world you will go where everyone goes, and no one truly knows where that is. The point is not to win or lose, but to play with ever-increasing skill.

Playing the game of life skillfully means playing without the illusion that you are in charge. It means playing with the growing realization that there is no purpose to playing, but that the playing is the purpose.

Knowing that you are here to play the game, you know what Ecclesiastes knows when he says,

> *For everything there is a season,*
> *and a time for every matter under heaven:*
> *a time to be born, and a time to die;*
> *a time to plant, and a time to pluck up what is*
> *   planted;*
> *a time to kill, and a time to heal;*
> *a time to break down, and a time to build up;*
> *a time to weep, and a time to laugh;*
> *a time to mourn, and a time to dance;*
> *a time to throw away stones, and a time to*
> *   gather stones together;*
> *a time to embrace, and a time to refrain from*
> *   embracing;*
> *a time to seek, and a time to lose;*
> *a time to keep, and a time to throw away;*
> *a time to tear, and a time to sew;*
> *a time to keep silence, and a time to speak;*
> *a time to love, and a time to hate;*
> *a time for war, and a time for peace.*
>
> (ECCLESIASTES 3: 1–8, NRSV)

54

You don't get to pick the time, and you don't get to escape the matter. You only get to play. And what is true for you is true for everyone else. No one chooses what happens to them; everyone is simply challenged to live what happens the best they can.

This knowledge should humble us. And when we are humbled, we have compassion for ourselves and others; we share (*com*) their suffering (*passion*), and forgive their efforts to live well when those efforts cause us more pain. Who's to say their actions aren't simply part of the season in which we find ourselves? Who's to say that the entire play isn't unfolding exactly as it should?

If you want to blame someone for your fate, do as Job did and blame God. And if you are as lucky as Job to actually have God show up and reveal the wildness of reality to you, I hope you will have the revelation he had—that you are part of the wildness and not apart from it—and that this revelation brings you the same comfort it brought Job: humbly surrendering to the unknown and unknowable, and finding comfort in that not-knowing.

Humility arises naturally from an honest appraisal of the fundamental wildness of life. When you see that life is neither controlled nor controllable, that what is rarely conforms precisely to your assessment of what should be, all arrogance and chutzpah dissipates. You stop making demands of life or of those with whom you live it. You realize that we are all doing the best we can with what we've got, and you can't ask for more than that from yourself or others.

The kind of humility I am talking about isn't a resigned detachment from life, or a depressed surrender to the powers that be. It is simply a recognition that life is bigger than us, and trying to control it is, to quote Ecclesiastes, like "chasing after the wind." And with this recognition comes a profound sense of serenity.

While you may not have read the Bible's book of Job, chances are you have heard of it and know the basic story. Job is a kind, just, and devout man who suffers the loss of his children, his wealth, and his health because of a bet God makes with Satan. Satan bets God that Job will renounce his faith and curse God as a result of his suffering. God bets he won't.

People talk about the "patience of Job," but Job is anything but patient. While he recognizes that God is the source of all that happens to us—the good and the bad—he is not willing to curse God for this (Job 2:9). Rather he wants to speak with God directly to find out why the innocent suffer. It would be more accurate to speak of the "insistence of Job" than the "patience of Job," and in the end his insistence pays off; God actually shows up and talks with him.

Job is convinced that a just God would not punish the innocent, and he would have been crushed to learn that his own suffering is the result of God's placing a bet with Satan as to how much suffering Job could endure before cracking and cursing God. But God doesn't tell Job the truth behind his suffering. Instead God appears to Job in a massive windstorm and peppers Job with cosmic questions as the sand burns into his already bleeding flesh:

> "Where were you when I planned the earth?
> Tell me, if you are so wise. Do you know who
> took its dimensions, measuring its length with
> a cord? . . . Where were you when I stopped
> the waters, as they issued gushing from the
> womb? When I wrapped the ocean in clouds
> and swaddled the sea in shadows? . . . Have
> you ever commanded morning or guided
> dawn to its place—to hold the corners of the

> sky and shake off the last few stars?" (*The Book
> of Job*, translation by Stephen Mitchell, pp.
> 79–80)

Job looks to God for answers, but all he gets are more questions. The interrogation goes on for a long time. At last Job seeks to silence God by silencing his own inquiries:

> I am speechless: what can I answer? I put my
> hand on my mouth. I have said too much
> already; now I will speak no more. (p. 84)

God, however, knows that Job is responding from fear, and does not let up. The questioning continues until Job has the breakthrough God desires for him. God is revealing the wildness of creation not to silence Job but to humble him, and in so doing, to free him from the notion that life should adhere to Job's sense of right and wrong, thereby freeing him to live with what is rather than continually suffer from the absence of what he imagines life should be. And living with what is, is the key to serenity.

Job's breakthrough does happen, and he says to God,

> I have heard of you with my ears; but now my
> eyes have seen you. Therefore I will be quiet,
> comforted that I am dust. (p. 88)

Stephen Mitchell's translation of Job's final words to God differs greatly from the standard English translation, "I have heard of you by the hearing of the ear, but now my eye sees you; therefore I despise myself, and repent in dust and ashes" (Job 42:5–6, NRSV), but his translation is truer to the Hebrew. Job doesn't despise himself: the word *emas* means to "regard as of little value," and suggests a state of humility rather than self-hatred. Nor does Job repent: the words *nicham* and *nichamti* appear nine times in the book of Job always with the meaning of comfort rather than repentance. Job doesn't repent in the dust, he finds comfort from the realization that he *is* dust.

Job sees God in the midst of the wildness of the whirlwind. But just what does he see? Remember Job is a broken man, covered in open and oozing sores, grieving over the death of his sons and daughters, and worrying over the loss of his livelihood. God is whipping around him in a blistering sandstorm. If anything, Job's eyes are blinded by the sand and are most likely tightly shut in defense against it. So whatever he sees isn't an external seeing, but an internal one. Job had heard about God with his ears; that is to say, he knew the talk about God that others spouted, but now he was seeing the truth within his own life and his own being. And what he sees is humbling: Job is dust. And what he sees is amazing: life is dust. And what he comes to know is comforting: there are no answers, there are only questions, and ultimately the silence to which all questing and questioning bring us.

What comforts Job is the realization that he is dust and hence not in charge of the universe. He is of the universe, which is itself dust. He realizes that he is part of God's vast and mysterious creativity, and the only response to this realization is a comforting humility. Job is free from having to make sense of the world, and free to make meaning in it.

If all this leaves you a bit dizzy, imagine how Job felt listening to God's questions. But hang in there. There is comfort in all of this.

CHAPTER SEVEN

Forgiveness and the Making of Meaning

WE BEGAN WITH the notion that forgiveness isn't an act so much as an attitude. And the attitude of forgiveness arises from our understanding of life as a wild and chaotic spinning outside our control. In other words, forgiveness happens when we realize that we are not in charge of life, we are only condemned to live it. Forgiveness happens when we realize that people are not out to get us, but out to take care of themselves. True, sometimes their caretaking causes us pain and suffering, but with the rare exception of the sociopath, our pain and suffering are collateral damage and not the point of their actions. The point is happiness.

We all want to be happy. Sometimes what we think will make us happy causes others to suffer. If there were a way to avoid this and still get the happiness we seek, most of us would opt for that. But the truth is that we are often unaware of the suffering our pursuit of happiness may cause, and are as surprised as the person we have hurt by the hurt we have caused.

Many years ago, in the middle of my thesis defense, my best friend went on a tirade about how I didn't believe a word of what I wrote and that my entire thesis was a sham. I stared at him in horror. Not only was his claim untrue, but he must have known it was untrue. Was he trying to prevent me from graduating? Was he jealous of my work? Was he so unsure of himself that the praise I received for the work I had done was somehow threatening?

As these thoughts raced through my mind fuelled by anger at my friend and fear that others would believe him, it suddenly dawned on me that whatever was motivating him it wasn't premeditated. I could see in his face that he was as surprised by his words as I was. He literally could not help himself. He stopped talking only when he ran out of negative things to say. It didn't take long, though it seemed like an eternity.

When he had finished speaking, the conversation resumed as if he had never said a word. I passed the defense, graduated, and moved on. And we are still friends. Neither of us ever mentioned the incident, and I doubt he even remembers it. But I do. It was and continues to be an important moment in my life. Why? Because it was an occasion for meaning making.

I have no idea why he attacked me, and even if I asked him to explain it, he would simply tell me a story that most likely has no relevance to the actual event. I bet he doesn't know any more than I do why he acted the way he did. Not knowing allows us the opportunity for making meaning.

What meaning I made of this incident was this: my friend was actually giving voice to my own hidden doubts. While I am almost certain that I never told him about the doubts I had regarding the positions I was taking, he articulated them eloquently. He allowed me to hear clearly the muffled concerns that were plaguing me internally, and in so doing he gave me a chance to respond to them. Not at the thesis defense, but later to myself. If there was any growth and learning in that thesis defense, it was from my reaction to his outburst rather than the praise of professors and peers.

I'm not saying he knew this is what he was doing, or that he did it to help me. On the contrary: I am certain he did it to make himself feel better. And if he was aware of hurting me at the time, I am also convinced that he didn't have a clue as to why he wanted to do so. My failure would not have impacted his success at all. He had nothing to gain from his outburst; he just couldn't stop himself. Something was happening inside of him that probably had nothing to do with me. I was simply the opportunity he needed to let loose whatever was plaguing him.

So I'm not suggesting that if you understand the inner struggle of those who hurt you, you will find it in your heart to forgive them. I am saying that you cannot know what is going on inside someone else; indeed, you may not even know what is going on among the subpersonalities in your own head. All you can know is that something is happening, and that something led to that hurtful tirade, and, chances are, the person hurting you hasn't got a clue as to why. It just happened.

FORGIVENESS AND THE MAKING OF MEANING

Did I forgive my friend? No, there was no need.
I don't believe he set out to hurt me. He had his own
madness to deal with, so compassion arose in me.
Also gratitude; my friend was inadvertently helping
me hear my own doubts. Knowing all of this allows
me to let go, to not insist he be someone he isn't, and
to continue to befriend him as he is. Without the
burden of having to make him fit my own needs, I am
free to focus on what really matters to me: my life and
how I live it.

Life doesn't come to us prepackaged. It is wild and
chaotic and filled with joy and horror and surprise.
Life doesn't come to us predetermined. Things happen
and we respond to what happens and our response
creates a new reality to which a new response is due.
Life isn't given to us. It happens through us.

If this is as far as our analysis goes, however, life
lacks purpose and meaning. It is what it is, and we are
what we are, and there is nothing more to say about it.
But there is something more to say, there is the story
we tell.

We are the stories we tell about ourselves. There
may not be a thinker behind my thoughts, but the
thoughts seem to weave themselves into a story that

makes me the protagonist. I may not be the author of my thoughts, but I am the editor that turns them into a story. The challenge isn't to control my thoughts and feelings, but to weave them into a story that gives me a sense of purpose and meaning.

Life doesn't come pre-storied. We have to make the story, and as we do so we create meaning for ourselves. The question is this: are you going to tell a story that casts you as the hapless victim or the courageous hero? If you play the victim you imagine that while you may have no control over life, others do. If you play the hero you know that while no one controls life, you always have the capacity to act with humility and compassion in the face of whatever happens. And acting with humility and compassion creates meaning.

Life doesn't have a preset meaning. Meaning is not something you inherit but something you invent. And you can't invent it if your life is mired in grudges.

As long as you are trying to figure out why a loved one harmed you, you haven't got the energy to figure out what to do next. And it is in the "what to do next" that meaning is made and life is well lived.

"Meaning" isn't some fairy tale you tell yourself to explain life. I am not looking for "God's plan for my life," or some meta-story revealed in the Zodiac, Tarot, I Ching, or entrails of a dead cat. Any story that explains life, explains life away.

I want to live life in all its rawness and not avoid it by blanketing it in some soft quilt of past-life karma or divine providence. When life is painful, I want to feel the pain. When it is joyous, I want to feel the joy. I want to live, as Ecclesiastes suggests, in tune with the moment. And when the moment changes, as it always does, I want to change along with it. But I can't do that if I am tied to the past and weighed down with past hurts and ever-present grudges.

This is why forgiveness is crucial to right living: it frees you from the past that you might engage the present, both good and bad.

If meaning isn't another story, what then is it? Meaning is the act of facing life courageously with compassion and humility. Meaning isn't a matter of content: "my life means X or Y;" meaning is a matter of intent: I live each moment with humility and compassion for self and others, and in this way of living I find life worth living. Moreover, living courageously with compassion and humility translates as forgiveness—forgiveness is how you live courageously with

67

compassion and humility—and by granting forgiveness you invite others to free themselves of constricting stories and write their own tales of courage, compassion, humility, and forgiveness.

CHAPTER **EIGHT**

What Is Forgiveness?

AGAIN: FORGIVENESS IS NOT so much an act as an attitude. As an act, forgiveness raises the forgiver above the forgiven; it empowers the one even as it disempowers the other. But in the real world there is no hierarchy of power, there is just the wildness of life and people doing their best to navigate it.

The act of forgiveness is a tactic, a way of getting through something or of getting one-up on someone. I know this isn't the way we normally think about forgiveness, but explore this with me a bit. If you don't like what I have to say, you can always stop reading.

The only way someone can hurt you is if you have given them power over you. When my son was a toddler and I refused him candy as we stood in the checkout line at our local market, he would often cry out, "I hate you. I hate you." While this might have been a bit embarrassing, it wasn't hurtful. He had no power over me, and his assessment of my character and parenting skills meant nothing to me. While you might argue that he should have apologized for his outburst, there is no need for me to forgive him for it. He just did what any three-year-old kid would do when forced to stand in an aisle stacked from his head to his toe with candy.

Now imagine a different scenario. You're standing with a friend who is under the misunderstanding that you have done her some harm. She too cries out, "I hate you, I hate you." Because you are innocent and because you know that she is misinformed you will most likely forgive her for her outburst, especially when she realizes her error and asks for your forgiveness. The difference here is that you have power over her. She was in the wrong, even if she didn't know it, and she may have hurt you with her anger. You bestow forgiveness upon her the way a governor may bestow a pardon on a criminal. Your friend humbles herself before you in asking for forgiveness, and you, with *noblesse oblige*, graciously grant her wish.

Forgiveness is yours to give, and in giving it you assert your superiority over the one forgiven.

Bear with me for a third scenario. Imagine you have hurt someone you love. He is angry with you, and his anger is making your life miserable. So you apologize, humbly and sincerely. Yet you expect something for this act of contrition. You expect to be forgiven. Your apology, no matter how sincere, is still a tactic. You want to be free from the guilt and the anxiety the other's anger produces in you, and so you own up to your mistake and apologize. If forgiveness is forthcoming you are freed from the weight of your guilt and free to reengage with the other person as an equal.

But what happens if you ask for forgiveness and forgiveness is not forthcoming? You get angry. Now you are the one who feels slighted. Now you are the one owed an apology. Now you are the one who has been raised, at least in your own mind, to the moral high ground: you occupy the superior status of the wronged.

When we focus on forgiveness as an act it all too often becomes a tactic, and a manipulative one at that. But when we understand forgiveness as an attitude something else altogether happens.

I expect to be hurt. Not all the time and not by everyone, but often enough by those I love that it isn't a shock—even when the cause of the hurt is a surprise. I expect to be hurt not because I think people are mean and hurtful, but because I know that people are most often victims of their own inner turmoil, and this turmoil just erupts now and again in ways that hurt me.

While I know there are people who set out to deliberately hurt others, I don't think I personally know anyone like this. I have some troublesome acquaintances and even friends, but none of them are sociopaths or psychopaths. They are just people like me. Often we are caught up in the madness of our lives in such a way that now and again we do something hurtful—often and especially to those we love. Welcome to the major leagues.

Does this mean I don't have to forgive them? On the contrary, it means that not forgiving them isn't even an option. This is what I mean by forgiveness as an attitude. Forgiveness isn't a tactic; it is your default level of engagement. You forgive because you know we are all trapped in our own madness over which we have no control. Not forgiving simply locks you into additional layers of suffering that have no beneficial results at all.

Am I saying that you should forgive everybody for everything they do? What about the person who mugs you or rapes you or murders your child? Are you supposed to forgive that person as well?

If I say, "yes," I am talking theory, and you should reject my ideas out of hand. It would be absurd of me to dismiss your anger and your grief over tragedies of this magnitude, and I won't do that. While it might be in your best interest to forgive even these evil people, I would not ask you to do so. There are no limits to forgiveness, but there are limits to forgiving. Follow your heart, not my philosophy.

If I say "no," then we have to decide when it is right to forgive and when it is wrong to forgive. But there is no way I can define this for you. You simply have to discover it for itself, and then have compassion on yourself when you do.

Could you forgive Charles Roberts, the man who shot up a one-room school house killing five Amish girls and wounding five others, if one of those girls was your daughter? Their Amish parents did. I can't say what I would do. Knowing that Roberts was the

73

victim of his own madness would help me move on without having to bury myself in hatred of the killer, but is that the same as forgiveness? Perhaps it is. But I am not going to tell you that you should or should not forgive Mr. Roberts. That is not my call to make. What I can say is that I will have compassion for you regardless of the choice you make.

But how many of us face this level of horror? So let's consider a lesser tragedy.

Over my twenty years as a congregational rabbi I have worked with several families of suicides. These family members are often very angry: with themselves—"I should have seen this coming, and never should have left him alone."; with each other—"How did you not see this coming? How could you have possibly left him alone?"; and most of all, with the loved one who committed suicide—"Why didn't he let us know how bad things were? Why didn't he reach out to us for help? Why did he do this to us? He's gone, but we have to live with this horror for the rest of our lives!"

All of this anger assumes a level of premeditation that most likely didn't exist. If you *could* have seen how desperate a loved one was, you *would* have seen it and taken action regarding it. If the person suffering so much pain that her only outlet is death *could* have seen another way out, she *would* have taken it. Most of the hurts we experience are not meant for us. They are by-products of the suffering others are feeling. The truth is that most of the pain and suffering we feel isn't directed at us at all.

EXERCISE #7: **THE EMPTY BOAT**

Imagine you are out boating alone on a lake. A fog rolls in and you decide to row to shore for safety's sake. As you do so, you notice another boat heading straight toward you. You assume the fog is blinding the occupants of the other boat to your presence, and you call out for them to turn aside lest they ram into you and perhaps capsize your boat. The others do not respond and their boat picks up speed as it homes in on you. You begin to panic. No matter which way you turn they seem intent on hitting you. You shout for them to look out, but they don't, and you are hit hard. Anger bursts through you and you scream at the others, leaning into their boat to make your point all the more strong. It is then that you realize the other boat is empty. Wind and current, not malicious intent, drove the other boat into yours. What happens to your anger?

If you're like most people, your anger disappears. It doesn't fade away or slowly dissipate; as soon as you know the truth it simply vanishes. Laughter may replace it, as well as a sense of relief; and you may even feel a bit foolish. But the anger is simply gone. Where did it go?

When I lived in Miami, Florida, I was once speeding through a school zone, unaware it was a school zone. A guy in a pick-up truck got my attention and told me to slow down, pointing to the school zone sign. I did, and yelled back, "Thank you!" He heard something else, and as soon as we passed through the school zone he started speeding after me.

Seeing him in my rearview mirror I was convinced he was going to pull alongside my car and shoot me. This was Miami, after all. I tried to out run him, but I couldn't shake him. Instead, I slowed down, rolled down the passenger side window, and let him pull up next to me at a stop sign. He was blistering with anger.

Before he could draw his gun, assuming he had one, I said, "I said, 'thank you,' not 'f-you.'"

I could see the anger drain from his face. He leaned in against his door and I thought I saw tears in his eyes. He told me that his daughter had been killed by a guy like me speeding through a school zone. We talked for a few moments and then waved to one another, and he drove off. Where did his anger go? Where did my fear go?

EXERCISE #8: **THE FRIENDLY PHONE CALL**

Imagine you are in a terrible argument with a coworker. You are filled with righteous anger and not reticent about expressing it. Mid-tirade your cell phone rings and you see it's one of your most important clients. You have to answer; do you allow your anger to pass from coworker to your client? Of course not. You pick up the phone, politely ask how you can be of service, or if you can call the client back, and, when the phone call is terminated, return to your yelling as if nothing had intervened. Where was the anger when you were talking

RABBI RAMI **GUIDE TO FORGIVENESS**

> politely on the phone? How did you get it back
> when the phone conversation ended?

You might believe that feelings like love and anger are stored somewhere in your mind and that you can put them down and pick them up as desired. I don't believe this. I think feelings arise of their own accord, triggered by situations beyond our control and retriggered by the stories we tell ourselves about those situations.

The anger in the father of the slain daughter didn't go anywhere when he realized I had thanked him rather than cursed him. The anger you felt for your coworker didn't go anywhere when you answered the phone. The situation changed and with it the feelings attached to it. You didn't have to control the anger; it was no longer present. It arose anew when you returned to face the person with whom you were arguing. But you had to rekindle that argument; it wasn't simply on "pause" as if you could freeze one story while you raced to the kitchen to get some ice cream, and then hit "play" when you were ready to return to it. No, you have to actively replay the story in your mind so that you can get angry all over again.

Why do we do that? Because we have told ourselves another story that says it is our right to be angry. Once we are convinced of that, we will replay the appropriate story to rekindle our righteous anger.

My point is just this: feelings come and go, but stories can last a lifetime.

There is no point to holding yourself or others accountable for the thoughts and feelings that come into your mind. There is no sense in imagining that you or they can always act contrary to either; you know you can't, so why insist that they can and should?

All you can know for certain is that life happens and feelings happen and thoughts happen and hurts happen and most of the time the boat is empty. Most of the time your suffering is collateral damage in another's struggle for happiness. You are not the target. This story is much closer to the truth than any tale you spin making the other a deliberate villain.

Knowing this, and telling this story, makes forgiveness almost axiomatic. The more we realize that we are simply caught in the wildness of life, the more natural asking for and bestowing forgiveness becomes.

EXERCISE #9: **THE CROWDED BUS**

Imagine you are on a crowded bus. The bus reaches your stop and you maneuver to get out. The bus is so crowded that you inadvertently step on another's foot. The person cries out in pain. What do you do? What does the other do in response to what you do?

When you accidently hurt someone this way you immediately say, "I'm sorry." This isn't a tactic. This is a genuine response to an inadvertent injury. Most often the other person says, "It's OK, forget it." Sometimes they say something else. When you say, "I'm sorry," and the other says, "It's OK, forget it," you are both aware of the chaos of life and the fact that suffering happens and the boat is empty.

When a person fails to do this, and instead launches into some tirade about how stupid and clumsy you are, chances are that person isn't so much reacting to you but to a story about being a victim of life's injustice.

I used to do executive coaching with CBS in New York City. During one winter trip to Manhattan I was racing to a meeting at Black Rock, the CBS head-quarters on West 52nd Street. I crossed the street, not waiting for the light to change and traffic to stop, and as I did so a car drove by and hit a slush-filled pothole, drenching me in dirty water and ice. I swear the driver did it on purpose, and for a moment I reacted with anger. But the car was gone, and I was drenched, and I still had a meeting to attend. What arose in my head astonished me. Rather than find myself in a fantasy argument with the long gone driver, I understood the moment to be an opportunity to see if I could simply respond to reality without any excess story.

Did I really know the driver set out to drench me in icy water? Of course not. Did I know he didn't intend to do that? No, I didn't know that either. In fact, I didn't know anything about him, or even if it was a "him" at all.

What did I know? I knew I was wet, cold, and dirty and that I had a meeting to attend and a job to do. Could I do my job wet, cold, and dirty? I didn't know, but I decided to find out. My life became an experiment. The only thing that mattered is what happened next.

What happened next is that I went to my meeting, told a funny story about New York drivers, and did my job. I created meaning by moving on constructively.

That is to say I chose to live meaningfully, to do my job to the best of my ability, regardless of the situation in which I found myself. This is all life offers us and all it asks of us—live well with what you've got.

So what is forgiveness? Is it an act or an attitude? I believe it is the latter. Forgiveness is the attitude toward life that recognizes how little control any of us has over what happens to us. Forgiveness is the freedom that comes when you realize how little freedom you actually have.

CHAPTER **NINE**

Forgiveness and Freedom

WE LIVE UNDER the illusion of freedom. We imagine that we can do what we want when we want, and that the only thing that stops us is our willful decision not to do it. This seems obvious enough, but when we look more closely we find this kind of freedom is an illusion.

Here are some limitations to my freedom: no matter how many art classes I take I will never be a great painter; indeed, I will never even be a mediocre one. No matter how much math I study, I will never be a great mathematician. I simply have no aptitude for art or math. The same is true of my abilities regarding basketball, hockey, tennis, and any number of competitive sports. I may desire to play well, but the fact is I lack the natural ability necessary to achieve my goal.

Does this mean I can't enjoy art, math, or sports? Of course not. It just means I won't enjoy them unless and until I accept my limitations regarding them.

Similarly, no matter how much I struggle to believe otherwise, my brain responds to sugar, fat, and salt in ways that compel me to overeat. True, if I don't indulge in sugar, fat, and salt, the compulsivity doesn't arise, but if I do, and I find it next to impossible not to, I cannot control the urge itself.

While we may differ in specifics, I suspect you are not unlike me: wish all you want; there are still some things you cannot have and some you can't avoid.

Does this mean we are robots programmed to be who we are, and lacking the capacity to be other than we are? I wouldn't go that far. I'm only suggesting that we have relative free will or functional free will, and not absolute free will. There are limits to what we can do and who we can be.

This is true of our emotional lives as well. There are certain situations that frighten me that may not bother you at all. There are certain situations that please me that may leave you uncomfortable at best. This is due to both nature and nurture, genetics and life experiences.

Within the parameters we are given, we have some room to maneuver. We can choose to act on thoughts and feelings that arise in our conscious minds, or we can choose not to, but we cannot control what arises. We can choose to create stories of victimhood or heroism, but we cannot choose to avoid stories altogether.

Is this real freedom? The question is moot: it is the only freedom we have. The wiser you are, the more subtle your capacity to work with reality becomes, but no matter how wise you are, you are never free from reality itself.

This realization is crucial to understanding forgiveness as an attitude. When we realize that we are all doing the best we can within the parameters of our lives, we are humbled, and with that humility comes compassion for the bad choices we make and respect for the good choices we make. Humility and compassion are the triggers that release forgiveness.

If you insist people are free—absolutely free and therefore absolutely responsible for what they do—you will have a difficult time forgiving those who hurt you. How can I forgive someone who deliberately and maliciously chooses to hurt me or my family if I am

85

convinced they could choose otherwise? Why would I forgive this person? My best course of action would be to distance myself from him, not to forgive him.

I'm suggesting something else. I'm suggesting that people who do evil are trapped in such a way as to make their actions anything but freely chosen. You can forgive them for their actions because they are not free to do otherwise. You can have compassion for their inner turmoil and entrapment; you can see where you yourself are struggling and entrapped; and so you can have compassion for yourself and the other. And that compassion manifests as forgiveness.

Forgiveness is an attitude rooted in the realization that the vast majority of people you will meet throughout your lifetime are doing the best they can with what they have. They are pursuing their likes, those things they imagine will make them happy; and they are avoiding their dislikes, those things they imagine will make them unhappy. All the while they are trapped in the delusion that they can actually get happiness rather than, as Thomas Jefferson wrote in the Declaration of Independence, merely pursue it. Nonsense.

You get what you get, and then do your best with whatever it is. Again to quote Ecclesiastes, "All things come to all people; the good are not privileged, and no distinction is made between the pure and the impure, or the pious and the impious. In this there is no advantage to being a saint or sinner, rash or cautious," (Ecclesiastes 9:2, my translation). Some centuries later, Jesus of Nazareth took the same notion and applied it to forgiveness:

> Love your enemies and pray for those who persecute you, so that you may be children of your Father in heaven; for he makes his sun rise on the evil and on the good, and sends rain on the righteous and on the unrighteous. For if you love those who love you, what reward do you have? Do not even the tax collectors do the same? And if you greet only your brothers and sisters, what more are you doing than others? Do not even the Gentiles do the same? Be perfect, therefore, as your heavenly Father is perfect." (Matthew 5:44–48 NRSV)

When Jesus says the sun rises on the evil and the good, and rains falls on the righteous and the unrighteous, I take him to mean that life happens to everyone, and there is no escaping good and evil. So love them all, because we are all stuck in the same madness.

But what does Jesus mean by "be perfect," and how might this shed light on the challenge of forgiveness?

When I ask people to define "perfection" they most often say something like "without flaw or blemish." God is thought to be perfect because God has no flaws. I find this definition, and the theology that accompanies it, less than compelling.

When Jesus is speaking about perfection he is talking about *shalem*, the Hebrew word for "wholeness" that shares the same root as *shalom*, the Hebrew word for "peace." He is saying, "Be whole as God is whole; embrace the light and the dark, as God is the source of light and dark (Isaiah 45:7a); welcome the good and the bad, as God is the creator of both (Isaiah 45:7b). Live life with that sense of peace that arises when you no longer race after likes and away from dislikes."Jesus is telling us to live with the wisdom of Job, learning to accept the good and the bad as natural to life, as coming equally from God (Job 2:9). God isn't good only: "I am the Eternal, there is nothing else. I form

88

light and create darkness, I make good and create evil; I the Eternal do all these things," (Isaiah 45:7, my translation). God is what is, both good and evil, both justice and injustice, both the welcomed and the unwelcomed. This is why Job says to his wife at the death of their children, "Shall we receive the good at the hand of God, and not receive the bad?" (Job 2:9)

When we understand perfection as wholeness, we see reality as including "flaws" in such a way as to allow us no longer to call them flaws.

Take the Japanese philosophy of *wabi-sabi*, for example. *Wabi* refers to being alone in nature, and *sabi* means "withered or worn." As a worldview, wabi-sabi refers to the beauty one learns to see in the imperfections and impermanence of life. Wabi-sabi sees perfection, the unblemished, as somehow lacking in aliveness. The perfect lacks depth and character. A wooden table that shows no wear—no dents, cracks, and bruises—has never been used. It has not known life and has never truly interacted with people. A wooden table with such "flaws" has character, and in that character is a real beauty that the new or untouched table lacks.

I am old enough to have had grandparents who

89

covered their furniture with plastic. The couch in my bubbe's living room, for example, was as clean and perfect on the day she died as it was on the day it left the showroom decades earlier. That's because no one had ever sat on it. Instead, we sat on a thick zippered plastic bag that encased each piece of the couch and its matching chairs. In the winter, the plastic was hard and cold. In the summer, it was sticky and mucous-like. But, damn, that couch was clean.

So many of us try to live our lives encased in plastic. We try never to get dirty, bruised, dented, or stained. But God rains on the bagged and the unbagged alike. To my bubbe, a stain on the couch represented a failure to achieve the perfection she deemed so important. To me, it is a reminder of some event that takes me into the story of my life. We live in our stories; wabi-sabi is a storyteller's pot of gold.

So if Jesus is telling me to live encased in plastic, I politely refuse. But he isn't asking that of me. He, like Ecclesiastes, is saying that there is no outracing good or evil, joy or sorrow. The key is not to be clean beneath a plastic bag, but to break the bag and live. And that kind of living means that you will hurt and be hurt.

Being perfect means being complete, and being complete means embracing all things and their opposite. If you want to be perfect as your Father in heaven is perfect, throw the plastic bag away and live with the humility that you suffer and cause others to suffer. And when you do, forgiveness becomes the very heart of your life:

> Then Peter came and said to him [Jesus],
> "Lord if my brother sins against me, how often
> should I forgive? As many as seven times?"
> Jesus said to him, "Not seven times, but, I tell
> you, seventy-seven times." (Matthew 18:21–22)

Forgiveness is never-ending, because screwing up is never-ending. Being perfect means being perfectly capable of doing great good and great harm. Being perfect means being perfectly able to repent as well as forgive. When we accept the truth of our nature, we are humbled. And when we are humbled we are filled with compassion, and when we are filled with compassion we forgive and seek forgiveness not as a tactic, but as a simple consequence of being alive.

Who Forgives Whom?

I HAVE DEFINED FORGIVENESS as an attitude. I have suggested that life entails hurting and being hurt. I have made it as clear as I can that realizing the nature of life is a humbling experience and that humility is the key to compassion, and compassion is the key to forgiveness. Life, humility, compassion, and forgiveness are all of a piece.

This may be as far as you wish or need to go regarding forgiveness. You might be saying to yourself, "OK, Rabbi, I get it and I've got it. We are all doing the best we can with what life deals us, and sometimes our best isn't very good and hurts others and causes them to hurt us, and nobody is really setting out to harm us; it just happens, so forgive and move on. But how? Give me some practical tips for forgiving."

I will, but not just yet. If you have had enough of theory, skip to Chapter Eleven and pick up some practical tips for forgiving others and for asking others to forgive you. But for those who can stand a bit more, I want to inquire into the very nature of the self that forgives and is forgiven. You don't need to read this chapter to learn how to forgive, but you just might benefit from it nonetheless.

Who is it that is hurt? Who is it that forgives? Who is it who causes suffering, and who is it that asks for forgiveness?

Earlier I suggested that thoughts create the thinker. This implies that there is no "you" inside your head that is running the show. "You" are in fact a by-product of the show itself. The question I want to pose in this chapter is this: are you a fact or an act?

Think grammatically for a moment: are you a noun or a verb? Most people think of themselves as nouns and refer to themselves as pronouns. Indeed, anyone who doesn't is thought quite strange as when Senator Bob Dole regularly referred to himself as "Bob Dole" rather than "I" or "me." Yet a noun is a static thing, and gives the illusion of permanence when in fact none exists.

EXERCISE #10: **THE DEFINING STORY**

Imagine you are sitting with your mother looking through photo albums of you and your extended family. Your mom stops at a picture of you at age four wearing a baseball cap and holding in two hands a first baseman's mitt far too big for one hand. She remembers the exact moment the photograph was taken and tells you the entire story of how you used to talk about baseball all the time, and that the only thing you wanted to be when you grew up was a first baseman for a major league team.

The story hits home. You never were good at sports, and have always felt bad about that. And now you know why. Baseball was your dream, one you failed to achieve, one that has probably haunted you subconsciously all your life. The more you think about it the clearer the notion becomes that you have never really lived the life you dreamed and that—

Just them your mom shakes her head and says, "Oh, no! No, sorry dear, that isn't you, that's your cousin Bob in this picture. He

wanted to play baseball; you always wanted
to be a garbage man, which is just what you
turned out to be. Wonderful, isn't it?"

What's happening here? Tied to the story, you were
about to fall into a great depression over a life poorly
lived. But it wasn't even your story. Guess what? No
story is your story; you don't have a story, at least not
the *you* you are in this moment. Stories are always
about the past, but the real you is only in the present.

Only nouns have stories, and the truth is you are
not a noun but a verb. You are a happening in this
moment; you are an ever-changing event. It is grammar that gives the illusion that you are a noun, but
when examined closely there is no "thing" that can be
called a noun at all.

All our talk about story had to do with the lowercase *s* self. Now let's explore the uppercase *S* Self. The
lowercase self is a noun, a character in a story. The
uppercase Self is a verb, something else entirely.

From the uppercase *S* perspective, we are all hap-
penings, and there is no "you" separate from what is
happening. Think of it this way: You see a woman jog-
ging in the park. Can you separate the runner from

the act of running? Is she a runner if she is sitting down or sleeping? If not, then what is the meaning of saying something like, "A runner runs"? If there is no runner who isn't running, the sentence is redundant. There is no runner separate from the running. There is only the running.

Let's take a look at this from another direction. Is there anything that happens to you, or do things only happen with you? If you believe things happen to you, then you can imagine yourself to be a noun separate from what is happening around and to you. And, better yet, you can imagine this noun self to be an innocent bystander, or even better, a victim.

The innocent and the victim have the moral high ground and can bestow forgiveness on the perpetrator of suffering. And the perpetrator can approach the innocent and the victimized as a supplicant and ask for forgiveness. But if you are part of the happening then this dynamic doesn't work.

For example, you believe your best friend has failed to repay a loan you lent her. She insists she did repay it. You know she's lying. She knows she's telling the truth. If there was some objective record of the transaction, we might be able to discern who is in the right and who is in the wrong, but lacking this, we only have competing stories. At this point you have two choices: you can forgive your friend for cheating you, or you can end the friendship.

The problem with either choice is that each is based on a story that you cannot be certain is true. But there is a third alternative: recognize that you are not the innocent victim of theft. If you had kept a record of the transaction this argument would not have happened. Or if it did, you would have concrete evidence that your friend is lying. She might persist in her lie, but that would only make it all the more obvious that she is trapped, a victim of her own madness. This fact could be used to forgive or forget her, but at least there would be no doubt. But you didn't keep a record. So you are complicit in the problem.

Here's the thing: you are always complicit in the problem. Once you know this and take responsibility for it you lose the moral high ground. You are humbled, and hence open to compassion both for the other and yourself. Admit your complicity and forgiveness is axiomatic. You learned something; now move on.

You are always complicit because you are always part of the happening, and there is nothing else but what is happening. If you were separate, where would you be? Where could you go? Can you go anywhere that isn't happening? Can you maintain the notion that you are a noun in a universe where everything else is a verb? No.

EXERCISE #11: **HUNTING FOR A NOUN**

Walk around your home or office and find something that isn't a verb: something that is fixed, unchanging, and permanent. If you look closely enough you will find nothing of the sort. Everything is moving, however imperceptibly to the human eye. And everything is decaying, however slowly. Walk outside and go noun hunting. You won't find one there either. Nouns are grammatical illusions not physical realities. Everything is a verb, happening along with every other verb. In fact, if you look carefully enough, you will see there aren't even a variety of verbs, but rather one enormous happening, happening in many ways in all places all at once.

The Buddha called this *pratityasamutpada*, dependent co-origination. It means that everything is connected to everything else and happens altogether. Cause and effect, therefore, is an illusion. Think about this: can you have a cause without an effect? No. If it has no effect it isn't a cause. Can you have an effect without a cause? Also no: if there is no cause there is no effect. Nouns, like "cause" and "effect" are grammatical maps that help us make sense out the wildness of life without ever really mapping that wildness at all.

Cause and effect arise together; each goes with the other the way back goes with front and in goes with out. One without the other makes no sense. The same is true of the forgiver and the forgiven. If this is true, and it is, then blaming someone for the drama in your life is ludicrous. You are as essential to the drama as the other person.

This is what the Self knows and the self does not.

The Self knows there are no nouns, only verbs. The Self has no story and knows the lowercase self is part of a story and incapable of living outside of one. The Self does not separate cause and effect, the one who hurts from the one who is hurt, but sees all things as a single dynamic, what the Vietnamese Zen sage Thich Nhat Hanh calls *inter-being*: things *inter-are*. The Self doesn't forgive or forget, it just doesn't stay still long enough for either to matter.

You are that Self. Or, better, that Self is you. But you are also the lowercase self, the storied self. It isn't a matter of identifying with Self and denying self. It is a matter of engaging self with the wisdom of Self. That is engaging each moment freely, without the story of the last moment, and being free to invent a story in this moment. The self is apt to invent a story of deliberate hurt, but the Self knows better.

The self forgives and asks for forgiveness as a tactic, a tool to be used to achieve the happiness the self seeks. The Self doesn't forgive in order to achieve, the Self forgives because there is nothing else to do.

Forgiveness is not a better way to live, it is the only way to live if, by *live*, you mean engaging each moment freely. The Self is always free; the self is never free. Does this mean the Self is free to do what it wants? Yes, but only because what it wants is simply to be with what is. The self is about control and manipulation; the Self is about being with what is humbly, compassionately, and gracefully.

The key to forgiveness is not learning how to forgive, but learning how to open the self to the Self, and move on.

CHAPTER **ELEVEN**

The Three Questions

WHAT I HAVE TRIED TO do in this *Guide* is shake up your notion of just what forgiveness is. Most people assume it is an act one bestows upon another. I'm suggesting it is an attitude one cultivates by looking more and more clearly into the nature of self and life. Most people assume that things are done to them; I'm suggesting that things happen with them. Most people assume they are who they think they are. I'm suggesting they are a by-product of thoughts that arise of their own accord, and that there is no thinker but rather an editor who files thoughts into habitual patterns to create a story that maintains the illusion of a fixed self.

If I am right, then there is no neat multi-step process to forgiveness. There is only forgiving as it arises from clear seeing in the moment. The instant you see that everyone is trapped, the moment you realize that the boat is empty, the second you know that you are complicit in everything that happens, you know that you are not in control, and you are humbled. Once humbled you feel compassion for yourself and all others. And with compassion comes forgiveness.

Don't mistake the limitations of grammar for cause and effect. I am not saying that first you see, then you are humbled, then you are compassionate, and then you forgive. I am saying that you live this seeing humbly, compassionately as forgiveness. Forgiveness is not caused by compassion; forgiveness is lived compassion.

So the challenge is to see clearly so that humility, compassion, and forgiveness happen.

What is it you have to see clearly? The truth that you and everything else are part of a vast and chaotic happening beyond your control. And how might you see this? By continually inquiring into the nature of what is happening.

At last we come to the programmatic part of our

Guide: something to do. I have kept this to the very end in hopes that by the time you got to this page you wouldn't need the advice it contains. I am hoping that you see clearly enough to just live forgiveness as a way of embodying the humility and compassion that are now inescapable.

But that presumes I write so clearly and so compellingly that you cannot help but see what I see and believe what I believe and live as I wish I lived. Make no mistake: I am as trapped as you are; maybe more so. The Three Questions I suggest below are three questions I ask myself over and over throughout each day. I share them with you because they work for me; that is they continually shift my perspective from self to Self.

Whenever something is happening (which is always), ask yourself three questions: *Who is aware of this situation? How am I complicit in this situation?* and *Who is in control of this situation?*

Who is aware of this situation?

Right now you are sitting in a chair or on a couch or lying in bed reading this book. Who knows this? It isn't the *you* that is reading because you are aware of that *you.* That *you* has a name, a story, likes and dislikes, and all the rest. That you is the lowercase self. But the you that is aware of this self has no name, no story, no preferences; in fact, it has no attributes whatsoever. It is simply awareness itself. This is the uppercase Self.

Which *you* is the real you? Both. Which is the freer you? The nameless one. The more you rest in the nameless Self, the freer the self becomes. The freer the self becomes, the less you suffer from the illusion of blame. Without the illusion of blame, there is no need for forgiveness as a tactic. Simply seeing what is happening without judgment, you engage the situation with humility and compassion, and humility and compassion are lived as forgiveness. You forgive because you understand the nature of reality.

How am I complicit in this situation?

The self is a character in a drama of its own composing. Because it has likes and dislikes, it knows vexation. Because it has a plan, it knows frustration. Because it wants some things and not others, it knows anger. And because it sees itself as separate from what is happening, it can play the innocent victim and blame others for all its problems.

Given all of this, when you are in a hurtful situation, ask yourself *how am I complicit in this drama?* What role am I playing that allows this drama to arise and continue? Don't take responsibility for the whole show, just your part in it.

This is not a "shifting the blame" exercise from the other to you, but a realization that, as trite as it sounds, it takes two to tango. Ask yourself: Why are you choosing to play in this drama? What are you getting out of it? How is it feeding your sense of self and self-righteousness? How is it fitting into and strengthening the story you tell about your self and your life?

The more you notice your own complicity, the more you realize that you and the other person are both trapped in the same drama. The more you realize the trap, the easier it is to focus on what you need to do to escape the trap, end the drama, and move on with your life.

As long as you fail to see that you are trapped in the drama, you will focus on the other person rather than yourself; you will expend your efforts on trying to change the other person rather than free yourself. You will focus on the idea of forgiveness, and how difficult it is to forgive this person given the drama unfolding, rather than end the drama and find that forgiveness is a by-product of your liberation from the drama.

Who is in control of this situation?

The answer to this question is always the same: no one. While the abuser may be more powerful than the abused, the abuser isn't in control of whatever it is that drives the abusive behavior. This doesn't mean you should excuse the abuser, only that you should waste no time trying to figure out how to live with him without triggering the abuse. Living with an abuser means that abuse will happen. Remember there are no nouns: an abuser abuses. Don't pretend otherwise.

How are you complicit in this? By choosing to play the role of the victim.

Am I saying that abused people have the power to just walk away? No, as long as they play the role of the abused, they have to stay with the abuser: their role demands it. That is why you have to ask the first question over and over again. In this case ask yourself, *who is being abused?* It isn't the observer, the Self asking the question; it is the self the observer is observing. That *you* is weak, frightened, and trapped, but the observer is none of these things. The abused cannot escape abuse, but the observer is never trapped in it. The abused self cannot escape; the unabused Self cannot be trapped. Rest in the Self and the self can walk way and seek help.

I am deliberately choosing the difficult example of an abusive relationship. I want you to wrestle with this. I am not blaming the victim, only suggesting that as long as one plays the role of the abused, one will suffer from abuse. When you shift from the abused self to the observer Self, you discover a freedom that the abused you has never known.

From the perspective of Self, you are not a victim, and you can act from your freedom at any time. An abused woman leaves an abusive relationship only when she opts for a new role. Until then she is always the abused. Identifying with the Self allows you to change roles whenever necessary.

This is a very powerful claim. Trying to free the abused from the role of the abused is like trying to bite your own teeth. It can't be done. The abused is by definition abused. The abused cannot change, but the person identifying herself as the abused can realize it is a role and stop playing.

You realize you are playing a role when you watch

109

the drama from the observer's perspective. This is Self-realization in which you discover the Self that is beyond roles and dramas. And from that perspective you can walk away.

The abused never has to change. She never has to overcome her fears; she only has to realize that the real Self is fearless and she is that Self already.

When you take refuge in the Self you are free to act in whatever way you see fit. You don't have to wait for a new thought or a better feeling. You simply do differently.

I have worked on this kind of observation for many years, and I can attest to two things. First, if you can learn to see your life from the perspective of the Self, you are free to choose to live differently. Second, most of the time you don't want to see your life from this perspective and be free.

It isn't that the Self sees more options for action than the self. It is that the self is living a story, while the Self sees reality as it is.

The abused self is trapped in a story that says she can never be free; one in which she blames herself for the abuse; one that insists that if she would only act differently, the abuser will act differently, and stop the abuse. It is a story of powerlessness.

The Self doesn't spin a story. The Self simply sees what is without judgment. It isn't a matter of who is to blame, but simply one of getting the self out of danger. The Self doesn't see the need to change the self, only to get her to safety.

This is true in every situation. The self is always a part of the happening, the Self is never so. The self imagines that it must change, grow, mature, become what it is not yet if it is ever to be free. The Self just says move on.

I don't have to learn anything about myself to be free from the things that ensnare me. I only need to see where I am ensnared and then walk away. To see this, I need to shift from self to Self by asking the first question, *Who is aware?*

But most of us don't want to be free. Of course we rarely admit this, but our actions attest to it.

Freedom places responsibility for your life on you, while you would rather place it on someone else. You want to excuse your poor choices by blaming someone else. If you forgive that person, the blame no longer fits, and you have to shoulder the responsibility for your life yourself, something you really don't

111

want to do. So you choose not to forgive in order not to be free.

This is no more true of you than it is of me. I can, at this very moment and with almost no effort, see where I am trapped in my life. I can see that the fears that keep me trapped are not impacting the Self at all. I am watching a version of myself that is afraid of change, but the Self that is watching is fearless. But as soon as I realize that doing differently is within my grasp, the frightened self throws a fit, I lose the clarity of my observer mind, and I stay stuck.

I am not saying change is easy. I am only saying it isn't complicated. Look and realize your freedom. That is easy. Then act from that freedom; that's the hard part.

We are like actors who refuse to drop our roles after the play has ended. We insist on staying with the drama: wearing the make-up and the costume and pretending to be what we are not. In time we may forget we are in a play. That's when everything in this book seems to be total nonsense. We are so identified with our roles and our play-acting that we cannot imagine freedom. We are so addicted to our thoughts and feelings that we cannot imagine an awareness that transcends them. We are so attached to our sense of self and self-righteousness that we cannot forgive; for to do so would put an end to the scene we are playing, and we are afraid to see what might happen next.

Let me lay a trap for you. If you have actually read to the end of this *Guide* and are convinced I am crazy and everything I have suggested is just so much nonsense, dare to entertain the idea that you are wrong. Take a risk and actually ask the three questions: *Who is aware of this situation? How am I complicit in this situation?* and *Who is in control of this situation?*

Forget me and forget whether my ideas are right or wrong. It doesn't matter. What matters is what realization you have when you ask these three questions: *Who is aware of this situation? How am I complicit in this situation?* and *Who is in control of this situation?* If nothing happens when you take these questions seriously, toss the book in the trash, or return it to the book store.*

113

---

* I prefer you toss it in the trash. That way I still get the royalties.

But if something does happen, if you glimpse even for a moment that you are not who you think you are; if you grasp for a second that you are nameless, fearless, and free; then read this book again until you see this so clearly that humility, compassion, and forgiveness are as natural to you as breathing. If I'm wrong, you have nothing to lose. If I'm right you have nothing to gain except the realization that you are free.

Forgiveness Month

THIS *GUIDE* HAS focused on our primary misunderstanding that forgiveness is something we bestow, and is written from the point of view of one who has been wronged. But what about asking others for forgiveness? This too is important.

Asking for forgiveness is important because doing so is humbling. Remember, humility and compassion arise together, and together they are lived as forgiveness. We have focused on cultivating compassion as a means of releasing humility, but in this final chapter I want to talk briefly about cultivating humility by seeking forgiveness.

I say "briefly" because there isn't much to this. When you sincerely ask for forgiveness you are sincerely humbled. So my concern here is not with theory but rather to suggest a powerful practice from the Jewish tradition called *Selichot*, pardon.

The final month of the Jewish year is the month of *Elul*. It is devoted to the practice of *Selichot*: approaching people with whom you have interacted over the year now closing and asking them for forgiveness. The Hebrew word elul means search, and the Hebrew letters of Elul—Alef-Lamed-Vav-Lamed—are an acronym for *Ani l'dodi v'dodi li*, "I am my beloved's and my beloved in mine (Song of Songs 6:3). The month of Elul is a month for searching out the beloved in every other, to recover the realization, as Zen master Thich Nhat Hanh put it, that all beings inter-are.

One way to do this is to admit that you have caused suffering and ask those who have suffered because of you to forgive you. Observant Jews seek out family members, friends, neighbors, coworkers, the clerks at the local bank, dry cleaner, grocery story, etc., and say, "If I have hurt you in any way knowingly or unknowingly, advertently or inadvertently, I ask your forgiveness."

Two things must be highlighted here. First, you don't admit to anything specific. Don't say, "Remember when I ran over your golf clubs and never paid for a new set? I hope you can forgive me." Maybe the person forgot about the clubs, or had no idea it was you who ran them over. By bringing up a specific case, you are forcing the other person to replay that story and may in fact rekindle their entrapment in their story even as you seek to get free of your own. The time to admit guilt was when you ran the clubs over, or when you are prepared to make amends and replace them, not a year later when all you want is to be forgiven.

Second, there is no obligation on the part of the person being asked for forgiveness to actually forgive you. Selichot isn't about manipulating them; it is about humbling yourself. It is the very act of admitting to another that you do cause suffering that humbles you, and with that humbling comes compassion for yourself and others, and with that compassion comes the capacity to forgive when asked and even when not.

Of course, you need not wait until the month of Elul to seek forgiveness. On the contrary, if you are following the teachings of this *Guide*, you will admit to faults and failings as they happen and seek forgiveness even more often than you bestow it, even if you forgive seventy-seven times. And yet there is something very special about setting aside a month of your life to ask for forgiveness.

If you are Jewish and live in a Jewish community, selichot practice is tough but not impossible. If you aren't Jewish and/or seek to practice selichot with others who aren't Jewish, it may be hard to explain what you are doing. Try, nevertheless.

We started this book with an exercise that turned Step Eight of the Twelve Steps on its head: thanking people for the suffering they caused rather than asking them to forgive you for the suffering you caused. We end this book with selichot, which is the Jewish version of Step Eight, making amends by admitting you were wrong even to people you haven't wronged.

Suffering is part of life, and so is forgiveness and the asking for forgiveness. All you are asked to do in this *Guide* is live: honestly, clearly, and constructively. In so doing, forgiveness will happen as naturally as breathing, and with the same result: ongoing life.

ABOUT THE
AUTHOR

BORN YIRACHMIEL BEN YISROEL V'SARAH in 1951, Rami spent several years in kindergarten trying to learn to pronounce his name. Being the only first grader who had to shave, Rami was promoted through school quickly, earning both rabbinic ordination and a Ph.D. Forced to get a job at age thirty, Rami led a congregation for twenty years where he learned that irony, humor, and iconoclasm made for poor bedside manner, and honesty was rarely the best policy when it came to religion. Author of over two dozen books and hundreds of essays, Rami writes a regular column for *Spirituality & Health* magazine entitled "Roadside Assistance for the Spiritual Traveler."